What does it mean to be

Blind

Louise Spilsbury

www.heinemann.co.uk/library
Visit our website to find out more information about Heinemann Library books.

To order:
☎ Phone 44 (0) 1865 888066
▤ Send a fax to 44 (0) 1865 314091
▢ Visit the Heinemann Bookshop at www.heinemann.co.uk/library to browse our
catalogue and order online.

First published in Great Britain by Heinemann Library,
Halley Court, Jordan Hill, Oxford OX2 8EJ,
a division of Reed Educational and Professional Publishing Ltd.
Heinemann is a registered trademark of Reed Educational and Professional Publishing Ltd.

OXFORD MELBOURNE AUCKLAND
JOHANNESBURG BLANTYRE GABORONE
IBADAN PORTSMOUTH (NH) USA CHICAGO

© Reed Educational and Professional Publishing Ltd 2002
The moral right of the proprietor has been asserted.

Designed by AMR
Originated by Dot Gradations
Printed in China by Wing King Tong

ISBN 0 431 13938 5 (hardback)   ISBN 0 431 13945 8 (paperback)
07 06 05 04 03 02   08 07 06 05 04 03
10 9 8 7 6 5 4 3 2 1   10 9 8 7 6 5 4 3 2 1

British Library Cataloguing in Publication Data
Spilsbury, Louise
  What does it mean to be blind?
  1.Blindness – Juvenile literature 2.Blind – Juvenile
  I.Title II.Blind
  617.7'12

Spilsbury, Loui

What does it
mean to be
blind / Louise
J612.
84

1459316

Acknowledgements
The publishers would like to thank the following for permission to reproduce ph
Photography: p.25; Trevor Clifford: p.10, 11(t); Corbis: p.22; Corbis Stockmarke
Format/Jenny Mathews: p.4; Sally and Richard Greenhill: p.23; Guide Dogs for the Blind: p.17; Last
Resort: pp.11(b), 14; Photofusion/Colin Edwards: p.9; Photofusion/Brian Mitchell: pp.15, 19; RNIB:
pp.19(b), 24; Science Photo Library: p.26; Martin Sookias: pp.12, 13, 16, 18, 20, 21, 28, 29; John
Walmsley: pp.5, 27.

The pictures on the following pages were posed by models who are sighted: pp.4, 7, 9, 11(b), 14, 16, 22.

Special thanks to: Biba and Frazier, Sarah and Natasha.

The publishers would also like to thank The Royal National Institute for the Blind, and Julie Johnson,
PHSE Consultant Trainer and Writer, for their help in the preparation of this book.

Cover photograph reproduced with permission of Martin Soukias.

Every effort has been made to contact copyright holders of any material reproduced in this book.
Any omissions will be rectified in subsequent printings if notice is given to the publishers.

Contents

Any words appearing in the text in bold, **like this**, are explained in the Glossary.

What is blindness?

What do you think it means to be blind? Many people think that being blind means you cannot see anything at all. This is true for some blind people, but not all. In fact, most people who are 'blind' can see something, though it may not be very much. It is difficult for them to see anything clearly. Being blind really means either that you cannot see or that you cannot see well. Lots of people prefer to say they are '**partially sighted**', which means that they have trouble seeing properly.

Only a few blind people can see nothing at all. Most people who have problems with their sight can see something. This is why the words 'partially sighted' are used nowadays.

People are blind or partially sighted for many different reasons. Some people are born with sight problems. Some people's eyes are damaged by a disease or in an accident. Some people have lost their sight in both eyes; others in one eye only. Anyone can become blind or partially sighted at any time of life.

Many children who cannot see very well go to ordinary schools alongside classmates who can see. In fact, you may be surprised to know that many blind children do most of the things that sighted children do. They may play football, ride a bike, write stories, read magazines, help around the house and even watch television. When they grow up, they will be able to do all the things other people do – go to college, train for almost any career they choose, and take care of a family of their own. Of course, some children may have more difficulties than others. Even so, most young people who are blind do not feel any different from anyone else and do not want to be treated any differently.

Most blind people don't let their sight problems stop them from doing the things they want to do.

How do eyes see?

To understand what blindness is, it helps to know a bit about how eyes usually work. Basically, the human eye is like a camera. It collects light from the objects you look at and focuses that light through a **lens** to make a picture.

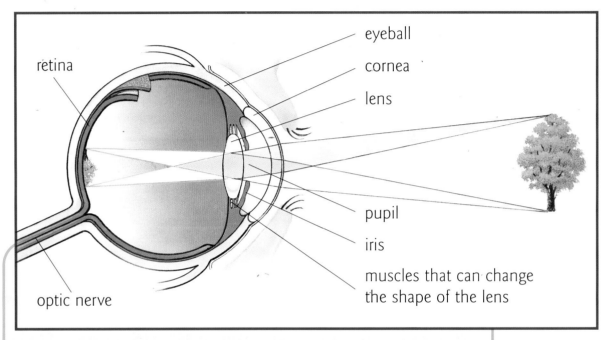

eyeball

cornea

lens

retina

pupil

iris

muscles that can change the shape of the lens

optic nerve

This drawing shows you the human eye, cut away to show the inside. When the image gets to the back of the eye, it is upside-down. The brain turns it the right way up.

At the front of the eye there is a clear cover called the cornea. The cornea helps the eye to focus (see clearly). The iris and the pupil are just behind the cornea. The iris is the coloured part of the eye. When we say someone has brown eyes, we are really talking about the colour of their irises. The pupil looks like a black spot in the middle of the iris. In fact, it is a hole that lets light into the eye. Muscles in the iris help to make it bigger or smaller in order to let more or less light into the eye.

After light has passed through the pupil, it reaches the lens. The lens acts a bit like a magnifying glass. It focuses light onto the retina, which is a thin layer at the back of the eye. The lens is held in place by bunches of fibres attached to muscles. The muscles change the shape of the lens so that it focuses the correct image onto the retina. They make the lens thinner when the eye looks at things close up, and thicker when it looks at things far away.

The job of the retina is to change the light patterns it receives into signals that go to the **brain**. These are kinds of messages that can be understood by the brain. The signals go from the retina to the brain by way of the **optic nerve**. The brain changes the signals into a picture of what the person is looking at. The only problem is the picture arrives upside-down! The brain simply turns the image the right way up so you can see it correctly.

In eyes that work well, the information about what you see reaches your brain in an instant.

What causes blindness?

People have difficulties with their sight for all kinds of reasons. Often, eyes do not work properly because there is a problem with one or more parts of the eye. For example, a baby may be born without the **optic nerve** (the part that takes the picture to the **brain**) having formed properly. Sometimes, a part of the eye may be damaged when someone is older. They may be involved in an accident, have a bad fall or get hit in the eye by something sharp.

Wearing glasses or **contact lenses** can help some kinds of sight loss. Some people have **operations** to help them see better. Once the amount of sight loss is known, the person, their family and their doctor work out the best way to help them.

Eyesight and old age

Most people who are blind are elderly. As you get older, your eyesight changes. Like the rest of your body, your eyes do not work as well as they used to. In fact, almost everyone who is more than 65 years old needs to wear glasses. Some older people find that they still have trouble seeing even with glasses.

8

Looking after your eyes

It is important to take care of your eyes, whether you see well or you cannot see very much. Here are some things to watch out for.

- Have your eyes checked by an **optician** every year.
- Never poke or put things in your eyes.
- Never look straight into the sun, or at bright lights.
- When you are reading or doing homework, make sure you are in good light. Make sure any lamps you use spread the light where you need it.
- It is not a good idea to watch television in a dark room or to sit too close to the screen.
- Don't stare at a computer screen for too long at a time, either. Try to take a break every half an hour or so.
- Always wear goggles (special glasses that protect your eyes) if you are doing metalwork, woodwork or any jobs where bits might fly into your eyes.

Bright sunlight can damage your eyes. Remember to wear sunglasses on sunny days.

What is blindness like?

Some people think that if they close their eyes tight they can get an idea of what it is like to be blind. This would really only show you what it is like for a few blind people. Most blind people can see some things, but they do not all see things in the same way. Some people can tell the difference between light and dark. Some can only see colours and not shapes. For some people it is a bit like looking through a tube – they can see only a small part of what is in front of them, perhaps just the bit right in the middle. Others see more of what is in front of them, but it may be blurry and there may be patches they cannot see.

The pictures here and at the top of page 11 show you what three different blind people can see when they look at the same scene.

Some blind people see a black blob in the middle of whatever they look at. The area around the black centre may look slightly misty or blurred as well. This is sometimes what elderly people who have problems with their sight see. Remember that everyone with sight problems sees differently, and what an individual sees may vary from day to day.

What is it like to be blind in one eye?

When you look at something with two eyes, it feels as if you are seeing exactly the same thing in both. In fact there is a tiny difference. Your **brain** compares these two slightly different views to work out exactly how far away an object is. If you have lost one eye, or you have lost the sight in one eye, you can still see perfectly well. It is just that you may have trouble judging distances accurately.

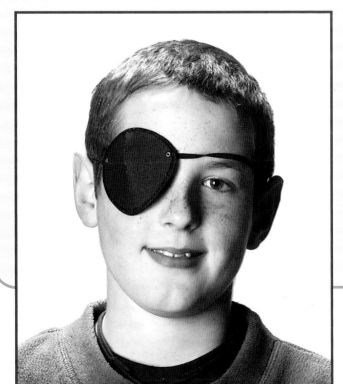

Meet Biba and Frazier

Hello. My name is Biba and I'm Frazier's mum. I've been asked to tell you a bit about Frazier. He is ten now. When he was about a year old I noticed his eyes wobbled a lot when he looked at anything and that he wasn't gaining weight as quickly as he should. Doctors found out that Frazier had **cancer** in his **brain**, which was affecting the **optic nerves** in his eyes. He had a lot of treatment to try to stop the cancer growing, but he has lost a lot of his sight.

Frazier goes to an ordinary school that has a **VI (visual impairment) unit**. He has lessons with the other children, but someone enlarges his work for him so he can see it. He has also just started to learn **Braille**. Sometimes he has someone sit with him to help him out, but usually he's fine on his own. One of the teachers from the VI unit takes him out for a walk once a week. He teaches Frazier how to tell that a car is coming just by listening, and how to cross roads. It's important for him to be able to get around by himself.

My name is Frazier. I'm ten, and I've got a brother and a sister. I share a bedroom with my brother, Miles. He is eleven. I've got a dog called Hamish. We had him from a puppy. He took quite a lot of training. Sometimes when you're lying down he climbs up and bites your ears.

At school, a different teacher comes to help me out in class. She writes the sentences down in big letters so I can see to copy them. I have paper with wide lines on it so I can see to write on it.

I like a lot of things. I like drawing best. I do paintings at home, too. I like to invent things and make things. My mum says I'm very inventive. I make clay models with that stuff that dries in the air, and I make models out of old boxes and paper. I also like history. I like visiting castles and other historic places like that. I like watching TV. I sit up close so I can see. I listen to stories on tape as well.

Everyday challenges

Think about all the things you do every day, at home, at school and in other places. How do you think people who cannot see very well manage to do all these things?

When you do not see very well, you become clever at using your other **senses** to do some of the things your eyes cannot do. Many blind people rely on their senses of hearing and touch more than sighted people do. For example, when a sighted person chooses what to put on in the morning, they use their eyes. If you cannot see, you can use your sense of touch to find the clothes you feel like wearing. On the way to school, people who can see look to check if anyone is coming towards them on the pavement. Blind and **partially sighted** people often become good at listening out to tell if someone is ahead of them.

People who are blind or partially sighted often use their other senses. They use their senses of touch and hearing to help them to find things they cannot see.

Some people who are blind or partially sighted may have other difficulties, too. For example, some blind children may also have difficulty hearing. They may need more help than people who have sight loss only.

Most people who have sight problems are able to do most things for themselves. They may need to use special equipment or have help to do some of the things they want to do. There are many different aids and gadgets that enable them to do anything from carrying out everyday tasks, such as schoolwork or chores, to using a computer. One example is the way blind people tell the time. When children who can see want to know how long it is until break time, they glance at the classroom clock or their own wristwatch. If your eyes do not work properly you can get special clocks and watches to help you tell the time. These usually have bumps where the numbers should be and hands that you can feel.

This girl is using a watch for blind people. When you lift the plastic top, you can tell the time by feeling the raised marks around the face of the watch.

Getting around

How do you find your way around if you cannot see? Most blind children find their way around easily when they are in familiar places. When they are at home or school, they usually get around by remembering where things are. They may also feel their way to help them. For instance, if you know your classroom is the third door on the right after the main door, you can run your hand along the wall and count the doorways as you pass. Sometimes your other **senses** can help you, too. If you can smell food, you should reach the dinner hall by following your nose. If you hear games being played, you know you are not far from the gym. It can be trickier in the playground, because people are always moving around, or they may leave their bags or coats in the way.

*If there is a blind or **partially sighted** person in your school, you could help them by making sure hallways are kept clear. For instance, if bags or coats fall off their pegs, they could trip someone up. Instead of stepping over them, hang them up out of the way.*

Out and about

It is more difficult when you are outside on the street. Roads are busy places and can be dangerous for anyone. There may also be lampposts, signposts, rubbish bags, bikes or trees on the pavement, which get in your way. Some blind people like to hold on to a friend's arm. The friend can guide them around obstacles in their way and warn them when they need to climb steps.

Some people carry a long, white stick called a cane. They move the cane left and right in front of their feet as they walk. This helps them to check there is nothing in their way. They also use it to feel the edge of a pavement or step. The colour of the cane tells other people that they cannot see very well.

Guide dogs

Some older people who are blind use guide dogs to help them get around. Guide dogs are trained to work as a blind person's 'eyes', and help them walk safely from place to place. They are taught to stop when they get to the edge of a pavement.

Reading and writing

People who cannot see very well read and write in a variety of ways. There is a whole range of different ways people can choose from, depending on what suits them best. Some people can see enough to read if the words in a book are bigger than usual. Sometimes their teacher may simply enlarge a worksheet for them in the photocopier so they can read it. Many blind children read by listening to cassette tapes. You can buy these tapes or borrow them from friends, schools or libraries. Lots of people who can see also enjoy these '**audio books**'.

Talking computers?

Some people who have sight problems use computers that can talk! When you type in a word, the computer reads it back to you. This means you can check what you have written before you print it out. You can also get special printers that attach to computers and print out the words in **Braille** (a system of writing used by some blind people), so that other blind people can read them, too.

Lots of books are available in large print. Look in your library next time you visit and see how many you can find.

Braille and Moon

Some blind people read by using their fingers. They read a system of writing called Braille. In Braille, letters and numbers are printed in patterns of small dots. These dots stick up from the paper so that you feel them when you run your fingertips over them. Braille letters are made of up to six dots, arranged in two columns of three. Different numbers and patterns of dots mean different letters. Some people write by typing onto a special machine called a **brailler** which prints Braille.

People who know how can read words in Braille very quickly.

Moon is another method of reading by touch. Moon letters are made of raised shapes based on the ordinary alphabet. Most people find Moon easier to learn than braille. You can write Moon on special paper using a frame and a ballpoint pen. Many people use Moon to write letters or messages, and some use it to write notes when they are doing their homework.

Moon letters are made of raised shapes.

Meet Sarah

Hi, I'm Sarah and I'm ten years old. I am blind because when I was younger I had **cancer** in the back of my eyes. I had one eye taken out in an **operation** when I was one year old. The other eye was taken out when I was five because the cancer wouldn't go away.

I go to an ordinary school. I do **Braille** on my **brailler** machine for maths and science. Sometimes a special teacher sits by me in lessons and helps with anything I cannot do myself. I used to write all my stories and essays in Braille, and she wrote over the Braille so my other teachers could read it. It took them ages because I like writing and once I wrote a story that was eleven pages long! Now I use a laptop computer to write with. I type on a normal keyboard and the computer reads out what I've written. It can print in Braille or ordinary text. At school, my favourite subjects are English and art. In art, I do a lot of collages and I like feeling the different textures.

I do a lot of writing on my computer. I write stories and poems. I've had four poems published in books. I listen to story tapes a lot. In fact, I've got four cases full of tapes! I wouldn't mind being a writer when I grow up. I used to want to be a vet, but it would be quite difficult. I love nearly all animals, except wasps. I've got a pet rabbit called Nibbles and a dog called Tara, who's quite old now.

I like to go swimming. We go every other Friday. And I like to play on the climbing frame in my garden with my little sister Charlotte and my friends. We've got a big garden and it's got a Wendy house in it. I go dancing on Monday nights – tap, ballet and line dancing. I like tap dancing best. I also love making things. My mum says, 'Give her a shoe box and she's happy for hours'. I make all sorts. I made a mouse house out of a shoebox once and I made a maze for my mum's friend's pet rat.

Living with blindness

This may sound like an obvious thing to say, but we are all very different. Some people have brown, curly hair and some have straight, black hair. Some people wear braces on their teeth to straighten them out, others wear glasses to help them see. In spite of this, some people are still picked on because they are seen as different.

If you are blind or **partially sighted**, you may have to wear very thick or tinted glasses. If people pick on you or call you names it is bullying, and it is right and important that it be stopped. However hard it seems to do, you should tell a teacher or other adult so they can sort it out. Sometimes bullies pick on people because they don't understand something. A boy called Richard, who wore a glass eye after he lost one of his own in an accident, was fed up with being teased about it. He decided to talk to his class about the accident, the false eye and how he used it. He even let people hold a spare false eye. After this, classmates no longer bothered him about it.

We are all different. Some people wear glasses, or have problems with their sight. We all just want to get on with our lives, and have fun with our friends.

Friends help each other. Livvi sometimes helps her blind friend Charlotte get around. Charlotte helps Livvi with her guitar practice.

Making friends

Some people feel a bit awkward when they meet a blind person for the first time. Perhaps you would like to make friends but are worried you will say the wrong thing. Relax – people with poor sight are just like you. Chat to them as you would to anyone else.

Here are some tips that might help.

- When you meet someone, it is nice to introduce yourself and say your name. This is especially helpful for a blind person, as they may not have seen you come up to them.
- Speak normally. Don't feel funny about using phrases like 'Nice to see you', as blind people use phrases like this themselves.
- Don't forget to tell people if you move away. Anyone feels silly if they are left talking to thin air.
- People who are blind do most things for themselves. Sometimes they may need help. If you think that a person who cannot see well needs help, ask them. They will tell you if they would like your help.

At school

Most blind children go to the same schools as their brothers and sisters and sighted friends. They have help from a specially trained adult, who works with them in the classroom. This teacher helps them to take part in all the lessons, and helps them to read and write using the method that suits them best. This may be using **large-print books** or **braillers**.

What about other pieces of school equipment, though? You have to see to use a lot of these, such as rulers and maps of the world. There are lots of special kinds of equipment for blind people, such as rulers with raised marks instead of printed marks. When it is time for maths, talking calculators can tell you what numbers you have pressed, and the answers to the sums you tap in. For geography, there are really big maps with raised parts so you can tell where things are by feeling them. With special equipment like this, children with sight problems can get on with the same tasks as the rest of their class.

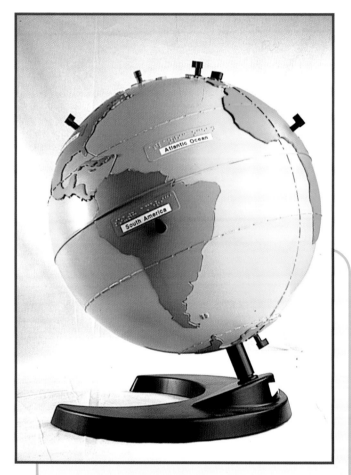

There are special globes for people who cannot see well. You can tell where countries are because they feel bumpy, and names are written in Braille.

Sports for all

It is good for all of us to do some sport or exercise. Doing PE or games at school helps to keep you fit and healthy. Most people with sight difficulties take part in different sports activities at school, although some people may need a little extra help.

Everyone can enjoy swimming. If you don't see very well, it helps if lane markers are brightly coloured so they are easier to see. It helps if lanes are clearly marked for athletic races, too. Before a race a teacher should also check that there are no obstacles in the lanes. It is important for blind and sighted people to know that they have a clear run.

In games, some blind people prefer to play in smaller groups, such as five-a-side football. They may play with a ball with a bell inside. The noise helps them to judge where the ball is. The goalposts are easier to see if they are brightly coloured. It is easier for any player to tell the difference between their team and the opposition if the two sides wear tops in clearly contrasting colours.

You don't have to see to dance well. Dancing is about moving with the rhythm of the music you hear.

At home

What do you do at home in the evenings, or at weekends? Whether or not you can see well, the chances are that many people's answers to that question will be the same – homework, playing computer games, playing sport or hanging out with friends, for example. Young people with sight difficulties want to do the same things as everyone else in their free time. Some blind and **partially sighted** people are able to watch TV by sitting up very close so they can see the pictures. Others can join sighted friends watching their favourite programmes by following the story through what people are saying. This is easier in programmes with a good storyline and where there is a lot of talking. It may not be so easy in programmes such as cartoons where stories are mostly told through pictures.

*You can buy many games that are made for people who cannot see well. Some playing cards have **Braille** markings so that people who cannot see and people who can see can play together.*

Helping at home

If you have sight problems, home is one of the easiest places to find your way around because it is so familiar and you know where things are. It helps if everything is kept in the same place all, or most, of the time. If you don't see very well, you probably keep your bedroom tidier than some people's. We all know how much easier it is to find things if they are always kept in one place!

Lots of household goods today have Braille labels as well as the usual ones. This makes it easier for blind people to choose the jar or bottle they want from the kitchen cupboard.

If things – from toys to kitchen utensils – are kept in the same place, you can do most things at home, even if you cannot see. You can help to clean the house and lay the dinner table, look after pets, and help with younger brothers and sisters. The kitchen can be a dangerous place for anyone if you are not careful. Children with sight difficulties find that, as long as things are always put back in the same place, they can help with cooking and washing up just like anyone else.

Meet Natasha

Hi. My name is Natasha. I'm nine years old. I've got **glaucoma** in my eyes so I don't see very well. It's hard to explain, but everything looks quite blurry to me. I can see things as long as they are big. My piano teacher blows up my music on a photocopier so the notes are big enough for me to see. The piano keys are easy for me to see because they are black and white.

At school, I have a helper called Frances. She collects me and walks with me to school. At school, she copies everything I need onto a computer and prints it out very large. If the teacher writes something on the board, Frances copies that out in big writing for me as well. Frances is great and we get on really well.

I write with blue and black pens as I can see them better than pencil. I write on paper with wide lines, three or four centimetres apart from each other. Maths is my favourite subject. My ruler is the same as everyone else's except it is yellow and green with black numbers that are easier for me to see.

I'm always busy. I'm in a theatre group called Chicken Shed. I go every week. We do dance, shows and acting. I'm best at acting and dancing. I'm learning **signing** for people who can't hear. When we have signing lessons, I sit at the front so I can see the signs, or someone sitting next to me explains what signs the teacher is making if I cannot see. I also go horse riding once a week. I can ride on my own at the moment. The teacher describes what to do in words as it is quite a big paddock and I can only just see her.

I love animals. At home, we have a dog, two cats, three rabbits and a guinea pig. I usually clean out the rabbits and guinea pig. I just know where everything is. Everyone keeps things in the same place. If I can't find something I get my little brother to help. I've got a baby sister too, called Hannah. She likes being with me. I look after her and even change her nappy.

Glossary

audio books recordings of books on cassette tapes or CDs

Braille system of reading and writing in which letters and numbers are printed in patterns of small dots. These dots stick up from the paper so that you feel them when you run your fingertips over them.

brailler special machine that types in Braille

brain control centre of the body. It controls the rest of the body, and how we think, learn and feel.

cancer serious disease in which the cells in the body increase very quickly. In many kinds of cancer, these cells form a lump or swelling called a tumour. Tumours can sometimes be removed in an operation, or they are treated in other ways.

contact lenses small, soft lenses that fit onto the surface of your eye. They help you to see, just like the lenses in a pair of glasses.

glaucoma disease of the eyes that can cause blindness

large-print books books in which words are printed larger than usual to make them easier for partially sighted people to see

lens transparent object with a curved surface which is used to focus light. The lens in the eye looks like a tiny version of the glass lens in a pair of spectacles.

Moon method of reading by touch. Moon letters are made of raised shapes based on the ordinary alphabet.

operation when a disease or abnormality is treated by doctors by removing, replacing or repairing the damaged part

optician someone who checks your eyes to see how well they are working

optic nerve nerve that takes messages from the eye to the brain

partially sighted many people who are blind have some sight, but not enough, for example, to read without large print or Braille. People with some (partial) sight may refer to themselves as 'partially sighted'.

senses the way in which our body picks up information from the world. The five senses are sight, hearing, touch, taste and smell.

signing using sign language. In sign language, people use their hands, upper part of the body and facial expressions to communicate.

VI units (visual impairment units) schools with special resources where people work who have special training in helping blind and partially sighted children

Helpful books and addresses

BOOKS
Living With Blindness, Steve Parker, Franklin Watts, 1989
I Am Blind, Brenda Pettenuzzo, Franklin Watts, 1988
Living With Blindness, Patsy Westcott, Hodder Wayland, 1999
Think About Being Blind, Peter White, Belitha Press, 1998

ORGANIZATIONS
The Royal National Institute for the Blind (RNIB) works for and on behalf of people with serious sight problems in the UK. For more information about the RNIB, its work and useful products, contact:
RNIB Customer Services
P.O. Box 173
Peterborough PE2 6WS
Telephone: 0845 702 3153
Minicom: 0845 58 56 91
Website: www.rnib.org.uk

For information, support and advice for anyone with a serious sight problem, please contact the RNIB Helpline, telephone 0845 766 9999 (for the price of a local call).

The Royal London Society for the Blind (RLSB)
Dorton House
Seal
Sevenoaks
Kent TN15 OED
Telephone: 01732 592500
E-mail: enquiries@rlsb.org.uk
Website: www.rlsb.org.uk

Sense
Voluntary organization working with people of all ages who are deaf and blind
Head Office, 11–13 Clifton Terrace
Finsbury Park
London N4 3SR
Telephone: 020 7272 7774
Minicom: 020 7272 9648
E-mail: enquiries@sense.org.uk
Website: www.sense.org.uk

IN AUSTRALIA
The Fred Hollows Foundation
Level 3, 414 Gardeners Road
Rosebery NSW 2018
Australia
Telephone: 61 2 8338 2111
Fax: 61-2-8338 2100
E-mail: fhf@hollows.org
Website: www.hollows.com.au/

Royal Victorian Institute for the Blind
557 St Kilda Road
Melbourne VIC 3004
Australia
Telephone: 03 9522 5222
Fax: 03 9510 4735
E-mail: iru@rvib2.rvib.org.au

Royal Blind Society of NSW
4 Mitchell Street
Enfield NSW 2136
Australia
Telephone: 02 9334 3333
Website: www.rbs.org.au

Index